Katharine Tynan

Irish Lovesongs

Katharine Tynan

Irish Lovesongs

ISBN/EAN: 9783744734462

Printed in Europe, USA, Canada, Australia, Japan

Cover: Foto ©Thomas Meinert / pixelio.de

More available books at **www.hansebooks.com**

THE CAMEO SERIES

Irish Love-Songs.

IN THE SAME SERIES.

JAMES CLARENCE MANGAN.

Irish Love-Songs

selected by
KATHARINE TYNAN

CAMEO SERIES

T. FISHER. UNWIN   PATERNOSTER SQ.
LONDON E.C. · MDCCCXCII ·

THE thanks of Editor and Publisher are due to the many writers and others who have contributed to this volume by giving permission for poems, their own or their copyright, to appear herein. We desire to make acknowledgment especially to Messrs. Chatto and Windus for the poem "I Made Another Garden" from Arthur O'Shaughnessy's "Music and Moonlight"; to Mrs. Allingham for her husband's poems, and to his publishers, Messrs. Reeves and Turner; to Mr. Aubrey de Vere and his publishers, Messrs. Kegan Paul and Co.; to Mr. W. B. Yeats, Mr. Alfred Graves, Miss Jane Barlow; and also to the proprietors and editor of *The National Observer* for leave to re-publish the two poems by Miss Tynan, and that by Miss Sigerson.

Dedication.

Take not my love-songs only that are made
            Ever for you,
But these more sweet that blew in sun and shade
            When all the world was new!

Take our wild songs, tender and passionate,
            Like those the blackbird sings
Beside some fairy rath, unto his mate,
            When all the world hath wings!

Take them, and think they speak my happy thought,
            My songs of you unsung,
These songs of many lovers, sweetly wrought
            When all the world was young!

APRIL 18, 1892.

Preface.

AMONG these Irish Love-Songs I have included
many that are not direct songs from a lover to the
beloved, but are rather songs of Love and the things of
Love. I have included also " Dark Rosaleen," the wild
and passionate love-song which the genius of Mangan
created upon an Irish cry by some bard of Elizabethan
days to his distressed Motherland. I keep it because it
seems to me the most beautiful poem of our Anglo-Irish
literature, and my book would be so much the poorer
wanting it ; and if any one is dissatisfied with this reason
he can figure it to himself a genuine love-song, as one may
conceive the Song of Solomon a lover's rhapsody to his
Eastern mistress. After " Dark Rosaleen," I believe my
little book will owe most to Edward Walsh and Samuel
Ferguson, the two men who, above all others, knew how
to transfuse the wild simplicity of the Irish songs into
English, keeping their strange and lovely flavour as of
wild bees' honey—sweet and unsophisticated. The love
for pure colour which the Irish possess is in these songs.
No one who loves poetry will ask what I mean when I

7

point to so crystal-clear and crystal-sparkling a verse as
Ferguson's—

> " O had you seen the Coolun
> Walking down by the cuckoo's street,
> With the dew of the meadow shining
> On her milk-white twinkling feet."

Most of these Irish poems date only about a hundred
or a hundred and fifty years back. Some are much
older, however, as witness "Beautiful Deirdre," from an
Irish MS. of the year 1400; and who shall say that
sophisticated nations, holding their Courts of Love and
all the rest of the mediæval frippery, could produce more
ornate and courtly praise of beauty than this? Poetry in
Ireland has a way of rising and falling with revolutions,
and there seems no doubt that the Jacobite movement
stirred into life the poetry with which the early years of
the 18th century in Ireland were rich. They were all
Jacobites, those shiftless fellows, who were the lineal
descendants of the bards, but, alack! without the bard's
position or his protector. Some were labourers, some
pedlars, some hedge-schoolmasters, all alike touched with
genius, wit, fire and learning—for it was a time when the
Irish peasant had the dead languages at his fingers' ends
—all alike scamps in a simple and virtuous age, and
adding to their scampishness a Voltairean spirit much out
of its due time and place. That those exquisite strains
of theirs owe much to the genius of Walsh and Ferguson,
is shown by the poorer figure they cut when translated by
Miss Charlotte Brooke, that first gleaner in the field of
Irish song, or by the translators in Hardiman's " Irish
Minstrelsy." Those wild songs have a certain family

likeness of manner and metaphor, but to me this cuckoo-note is but an added charm. They did not take kindly to the fine English of their first translators, who would dress them *à la mode*. How delightfully the Irish Muse of the date could prank herself in finery one sees in the lyrics of the Hon. George Ogle and like gentlemen. The " Banks of Banna " has a kinship, to my mind, with the delicate music of Purcell and Arne. I have selected for my little book arbitrarily, and have rejected many who in a larger collection would be honourably represented. I have sometimes rejected, but not always, because of an English influence, having the desire to make a book of Love-Songs of a new flavour, and literary in a fresh way. In this ambition I hope I have succeeded. And in conclusion, with my book, I offer to all English-speaking lovers Greeting !

KATHARINE TYNAN.

Contents.

❧

11

The Banks of Banna.

HON. GEORGE OGLE.

SHEPHERDS, I have lost my love,
  Have you seen my Anna?
Pride of every shady grove
  On the Banks of Banna.
I for her my home forsook,
  Near yon misty mountain ;
Left my flocks, my pipe, my crook,
  Greenwood shade and fountain.

Never shall I see them more
  Until her returning ;
All the joys of life are o'er,
  Gladness changed to mourning.
Whither is my charmer flown?
  Shepherds, tell me whither?
Woe is me ! perhaps she's gone
  For ever and for ever.

15

Molly Asthore.

HON. GEORGE OGLE.

AS down by Banna's banks I strayed, one evening in
    May,
The little birds with blithest notes made vocal every
    spray ;
They sung their little notes of love, they sung them o'er
    and o'er :
Ah, gramachree, ma colleen oge, ma Molly Asthore !

The daisies pied and all the sweets the dawn of Nature
    yields,
The primrose pale, the violet blue, lay scattered o'er the
    fields :
Such fragrance in the bosom lies of her whom I adore,
Ah, gramachree, ma colleen oge, ma Molly Asthore !

I laid me down upon a bank bewailing my sad fate,
That doomed me thus the slave of Love and cruel Molly's
    hate.
How can she break the honest heart that wears her in its
    core ?
Ah, gramachree, ma colleen oge, ma Molly Asthore !

You said you loved me, Molly dear; ah, why did I
   believe?
Yet who could think such tender words were meant but
   to deceive.
That love was all I asked on earth; nay, Heaven could
   give no more,
Ah, gramachree, ma colleen oge, ma Molly Asthore!

Oh, had I all the flocks that graze on yonder yellow hill,
Or lowed for me the numerous herds that yon green pas-
   tures fill;
With her I'd gladly share my kine, with her my fleecy
   store,
Ah, gramachree, ma colleen oge, ma Molly Asthore!

Two turtle doves above my head sat courting on a bough,
I envied them their happiness to see them bill and coo:
Such fondness once for me she showed, but now, alas, 'tis
   o'er!
Ah, gramachree, ma colleen oge, ma Molly Asthore!

Then fare thee well, my Molly dear! thy loss I e'er shall
   moan,
While life remains in Strephon's heart it beats for thee
   alone;
Though thou art false may heaven on thee its choicest
   blessings pour,
Ah, gramachree, ma colleen oge, ma Molly Asthore.

Love Song.

GEORGE DARLEY.

SWEET in her green dell the flower of beauty slumbers,
  Lulled by the faint breezes sighing through her
    hair ;
Sleeps she and hears not the melancholy numbers
  Breathed to my sad lute 'mid the lonely air.

Down from the high cliffs the rivulet is teeming
  To wind round the willow banks that lure him from
    above ;
O that in tears, from my rocky prison streaming,
  I too could glide to the bower of my love !

Ah, where the woodbines with sleepy arms have wound
    her,
  Opes she her eyelids at the dream of my lay,
Listening, like the dove, while the fountains echo round
    her,
  To her lost mate's call in the forests far away.

Come then, my bird ! For the peace thou ever bearest,
  Still heaven's messenger of comfort to me,
Come, this fond bosom, O faithfulest and fairest
  Bleeds with its death-wound its wound of love for
    thee !

Kathleen O'More.

GEORGE NUGENT REYNOLDS.

MY love, still I think that I see her once more,
But alas ! she has left me her loss to deplore,
My own little Kathleen, my poor little Kathleen,
My Kathleen O'More !

Her hair glossy black, her eyes were dark blue,
Her colour still changing, her smiles ever new—
So pretty was Kathleen, my sweet little Kathleen,
My Kathleen O'More !

She milked the dun cow that ne'er offered to stir ;
Though wicked to all it was gentle to her—
So kind was my Kathleen, my poor little Kathleen,
My Kathleen O'More !

She sat at the door one cold afternoon,
To hear the wind blow and to gaze on the moon
So pensive was Kathleen, my poor little Kathleen
My Kathleen O'More !

Cold was the night-breeze that sighed round her bower,
It chilled my poor Kathleen, she drooped from that hour,
    And I lost my poor Kathleen, my own little Kathleen,
        My Kathleen O'More.

The bird of all birds that my heart loves the best,
Is the robin that in the churchyard builds his nest ;
    For he seems to watch Kathleen, hops lightly o'er
        Kathleen,
            My Kathleen O'More !

Shule Aroon.

A BRIGADE BALLAD.

I WOULD I were on yonder hill,
    'Tis there I'd sit and cry my fill,
Till every tear would turn a mill,
    Is go d-teidh tu, a mhúirnin! slán.

Chor. —Siubhail, Siubhail a rúin !
    Siubhail go socair, agus siubhail go ciùin,
    Siubhail go d-ti an doras agus eulaigh liom,
    Is go d-teidh tu, a mhúirnin ! slán.[1]

I'll sell my rock, I'll sell my reel,
I'll sell my only spinning-wheel,
To buy for my love a sword of steel,
Is go d-teidh tu, a mhúirnin ! slán.

I'll dye my petticoats, I'll dye them red,
And round the world I'll beg my bread,
Until my parents shall wish me dead,
Is go d'teidh tu, a mhúirnin ! slán.

I wish, I wish, I wish in vain,
I wish I had my heart again,
And vainly think I'd not complain,
Is go d-teidh tu, a mhúirnin ! slán.

But now my love has gone to France
To try his fortune to advance ;
If he e'er come back tis but a chance,
Is go d-teidh tu, a mhúirnin ! slán.

[1] " Move, move, move, O treasure,
    Move quietly and move gently,
    Move to the door and elope with me,
    And may'st thou go, O darling, safe."

The Desmond.

THOMAS MOORE.

BY the Feal's wave benighted,
No star in the skies,
To thy door by Love lighted
I first saw those eyes,
Some voice whispered o'er me
As the threshold I crost,
There was ruin before me,
If I loved I was lost.

Love came, and brought sorrow
Too soon in his train ;
Yet so sweet that to-morrow
'Twere welcome again.
Though misery's full measure
My portion should be,
I would drain it with pleasure
If poured out by thee.

You who call it dishonour
To bow to this flame,
If you've eyes, look upon her
And blush while you blame.

Hath the pearl less whiteness,
      Because of its birth?
Hath the violet less brightness
      For growing near earth?

No; man for his glory
      To ancestry flies,
But woman's bright story
      Is told in her eyes.
While the monarch but traces
      Through mortals his line,
Beauty, born of the graces,
      Ranks next to Divine!

Kitty of Coleraine.

AS beautiful Kitty one morning was tripping
      With a pitcher of milk from the fair of Coleraine,
When she saw me she stumbled, the pitcher down
      tumbled,
      And all the sweet buttermilk watered the plain.
Oh! what shall I do now? 'Twas looking at you, now;
      Sure, sure, such a pitcher I'll ne'er meet again;
'Twas the pride of my dairy! O Barney O'Cleary,
      You're sent as a plague to the girls of Coleraine!

I sat down beside her, and gently did chide her,
   That such a misfortune should give her such pain ;
A kiss then I gave her, and ere I did leave her,
   She vowed for such pleasure she'd break it again.
'Twas haymaking season—I can't tell the reason—
   Misfortunes will never come single 'tis plain ;
For very soon after poor Kitty's disaster
   The devil a pitcher was whole in Coleraine.

Savourneen Deelish.

ANON.

Ah ! the moment was sad when my love and I parted,
   Savourneen deelish, Eileen Oge !
As I kissed off her tears, I was nigh broken-hearted,
   Savourneen deelish, Eileen Oge !
Wan was her cheek when she hung on my shoulder,
Damp was her hand, no marble was colder,
I felt that I never again should behold her,
   Savourneen deelish, Eileen Oge !

When the word of command put our men into motion,
   Savourneen deelish, Eileen Oge !
I buckled on my knapsack to cross the wide ocean,
   Savourneen deelish, Eileen Oge !

Brisk were our troops—all roaring like thunder,
Pleased with the voyage, impatient for plunder,
My bosom with grief well-nigh torn was asunder,
    Savourneen deelish, Eileen Oge !

Long I fought for my country, far, far from my true love,
    Savourneen deelish, Eileen Oge !
All my pay and my booty I hoarded for you, love,
    Savourneen deelish, Eileen Oge !
Peace was proclaimed : escaped from the slaughter,
Landed at home, my sweet girl, I sought her ;
But sorrow, alas ! to the cold grave had brought her,
    Savourneen deelish, Eileen Oge !

Ellen Bawn.

JAMES CLARENCE MANGAN.

ELLEN BAWN, O Ellen Bawn, you darling, darling,
    dear, you,
Sit awhile beside me here, I'll die unless I'm near you !
'Tis for you I'd swim the Suir and breast the Shannon's
    waters ;
For Ellen, dear, there's not your peer in Galway's bloom-
    ing daughters !

Had I Limerick's gems and gold at will to mete and
    measure,
Were Loughrea's abundance mine and all Portumna's
    treasure,
These might lure me, might insure me many and many
    new love,
But O ! no bribe could pay your tribe for one like you,
    my true love.

Blessings be on Connaught ! that's the place for sport
    and raking !
Blessings, too, my love, on you a-sleeping and a-waking !
I'd have met you, dearest Ellen, when the sun went
    under,
But woe ! the flooding Shannon broke across my path in
    thunder.

Ellen, I'd give all the deer in Limerick's parks and
    arbours,
Aye, and all the ships that rode last year in Munster's
    harbours,
Could I blot from Time the hour I first became your lover,
For O, you've given my heart a wound it never can
    recover.

Would to God that in the sod my corpse to-night were
    lying,
And the wild birds wheeling o'er it, and the winds
    a-sighing,
Since your cruel mother and your kindred chose to sever
Two hearts that Love would blend in one for ever and
    for ever.

Dark Rosaleen.

(From the Irish.)

JAMES CLARENCE MANGAN.

O MY Dark Rosaleen
    Do not sigh, do not weep !
The priests are on the ocean green,
    They march along the deep.
There's wine from the royal Pope,
    Upon the ocean green ;
And Spanish ale shall give you hope
    My Dark Rosaleen !
    My own Rosaleen !
Shall glad your heart, shall give you hope,
Shall give you health, and help, and hope,
    My Dark Rosaleen !

Over hills and through dales,
    Have I roamed for your sake ;
All yesterday I sailed with sails
    On river and on lake.
The Erne, at its highest flood,
    I dashed across unseen,

For there was lightning in my blood,
    My Dark Rosaleen
    My own Rosaleen !
O there was lightning in my blood,
Red lightning lightened through my blood,
    My Dark Rosaleen !

All day long in unrest
    To and fro do I move,
The very heart within my breast
    Is wasted for you, Love !
The heart in my bosom faints
    To think of you, my queen !
My life of life, my saint of saints,
    My Dark Rosaleen !
    My own Rosaleen !
To hear your sweet and sad complaints,
My life, my love, my saint of saints,
    My Dark Rosaleen !

Woe and pain, pain and woe,
    Are my lot night and noon ;
To see your bright face clouded so,
    Like to the mournful moon.
But yet will I rear your throne
    Again in golden sheen :
'Tis you shall reign, shall reign alone,
    My Dark Rosaleen !
    My own Rosaleen !
'Tis you shall have the golden throne,
'Tis you shall reign, and reign alone,
    My Dark Rosaleen !

Over dews, over sands,
     Will I fly for your weal :
Your holy, delicate white hands
     Shall girdle me with steel.
At home, in your emerald bowers,
     From morning's dawn till e'en,
You'll pray for me, my flower of flowers,
     My Dark Rosaleen !
     My fond Rosaleen !
You'll think of me through daylight's hours,
My virgin flower, my flower of flowers,
     My Dark Rosaleen !

I could scale the blue air,
     I could plough the high hills,
Oh, I could kneel all night in prayer,
     To heal your many ills.
And one beamy smile from you
     Would float like light between
My toils and me, my own, my true,
     My Dark Rosaleen !
     My fond Rosaleen !
Would give me life and soul anew,
A second life, a soul anew,
     My Dark Rosaleen !

O ! the Erne shall run red
     With redundance of blood,
The earth shall rock beneath our tread,
     And flames wrap hill and wood,

And gun-peal, and slogan-cry,
  Wake many a glen serene,
Ere you shall fade, ere you shall die,
  My Dark Rosaleen !
  My own Rosaleen !
The Judgment Hour must first be nigh,
Ere you can fade, ere you can die,
  My Dark Rosaleen !

Blooming Deirdre.

(From the Irish.)

EDWARD LAWSON.

SWEET Deirdre o'er all else I prize,
  Her pearly teeth, her azure eyes ;
O'er which, dispersed by the wind's play,
Dark, shining, twining ringlets stray,
In full luxuriant wreaths descending
Those small, soft-heaving orbs defending
Whose vestal snow no touch profane
Of man has ever dared to stain.

Like orient Venus when she presses
The brine from her ambrosial tresses,
That down her sleek side glittering flow
Like dew-stars on a rose of snow.

The dreary tenants of the tide,
With wondering gaze forget to glide ;
Suspended in the liquid sky,
The plumèd song-birds cease to fly,
Chorusing her praise to heaven above,
Where she'd depose the Queen of Love.

Hopeless I pine, accusing death,
Whose barbarous shafts still spare my breath,
A martyr to protracted anguish,
Like joyless, sapless age I languish ;
Nor read a line nor tune an air.
Over my head shuts in despair.

The Coolun.[1]

(From the Irish.)

SIR SAMUEL FERGUSON.

OH, had you seen the Coolun
    Walking down by the cuckoo's street,
With the dew of the meadow shining
    On her milk-white twinkling feet.

[1] *Coolun*, the flowing love-locks of the native Irish, applied as a term of fondness to those endowed with beautiful hair.

O my love she is and my colleen oge,
And she dwells in Balnagar ;
And she bears the palm of beauty bright
From the fairest that in Erin are.

In Balnagar is the Coolun,
Like the berry on the bough her cheek ;
Bright beauty dwells for ever
On her fair neck and ringlets sleek.
O sweeter is her mouth's soft music
Than the lark or thrush at dawn,
Or the blackbird in the greenwood singing
Farewell to the setting sun.

Rise up, my boy, make ready
To horse, for I forth would ride,
To follow the modest damsel
Where she walks on the green hill-side ;
For ever since our youth were we plighted
In faith, truth, and wedlock true.
O sweeter her voice is nine times over
Than organ or cuckoo !

And ever since my childhood
I've loved the fair and darling child ;
But our people came between us,
And with lucre our pure love defiled.
Oh, my woe it is and my bitter pain,
And I weep it night and day
That the colleen bawn of my early love
Is torn from my heart away.

Cean Dubh Deelish.[1]

SIR SAMUEL FERGUSON.

PUT your head, darling, darling, darling,
  Your darling black head my heart above ;
Oh, mouth of honey, with the thyme for fragrance,
  Who with heart in breast could deny you love ?

Oh, many and many a young girl for me is pining,
  Letting her locks of gold to the cold wind free,
For me the foremost of our gay young fellows ;
  But I'd leave a hundred, pure love, for thee !

Then put your head, darling, darling, darling,
  Your darling black head my heart above ;
Oh, mouth of honey, with the thyme for fragrance,
  Who, with heart in breast, could deny you love ?

[1] Pronounced *Cawn dhu deelish*, *i.e.*, dear black head.

The Lapful of Nuts.

SIR SAMUEL FERGUSON.

WHENE'ER I see soft hazel eyes
    And nut-brown curls,
I think of those bright days I spent
    Among the Limerick girls;
When up through Cratla woods I went
    Nutting with thee ;
And we plucked the glossy clustering fruit
    From many a bending tree.

Beneath the hazel boughs we sat,
    Thou, love, and I,
And the gathered nuts lay in thy lap,
    Beneath thy downcast eye ;
But little we thought of the store we'd won,
    I, love, or thou ;
For our hearts were full, and we dare not own
    The love that's spoken now.

Oh, there's wars for willing hearts in Spain,
    And high Germanie !
And I'll come back, ere long, again
    With knightly fame and fee :
And I'll come back, if I ever come back,
    Faithful to thee,
That sat with thy white lap full of nuts,
    Beneath the hazel tree.

The Fair-haired Girl.

(Irish Song.)

SIR SAMUEL FERGUSON.

THE sun has set, the stars are still,
   The red moon hides behind the hill;
The tide has left the brown beach bare,
The birds have fled the upper air;
Upon her branch the lone cuckoo
Is chanting still her sad adieu;
And you, my fair-haired girl, must go
Across the salt sea under woe!

I through love have learned three things:
Sorrow, sin, and death it brings;
Yet day by day my heart within
Dares shame and sorrow, death and sin:
Maiden, you have aimed the dart,
Rankling in my ruined heart:
Maiden, may the God above
Grant you grace to grant me love!

Sweeter than the viol's string,
And the notes that blackbirds sing;
Brighter than the dewdrops rare
Is the maiden wondrous fair:

Like the silver swans at play
Is her neck as bright as day !
Woe is me that e'er my sight
Dwelt on charms so deadly bright !

Nora of the Amber Hair.

(From the Irish.)

SIR SAMUEL FERGUSON.

O NORA, amber-coolun,
   It robs me of my rest,
That my head should be forbidden
   To lie upon thy breast !
It robs me of my rest, Love,
   And it breaks my heart and brain ;
And oh ! that I could bear my dear
   Across the raging main !

Oh, valentine and sweetheart !
   Be true to what you swore
When you promised me you'd marry me
   Without a farthing store ;
Oh, we'd walk the dew together,
   And light our steps should be ;
And Nora, amber-coolun,
   I'd kiss you daintily.

Hard by the holm
    Lives this white love of mine ;
Her thick hair's like amber,
    Which causes me to pine.
King of the Sabbath,
    Oh, grant me soon to see
My own fat cattle grazing
    Around sweet Ballybuy !

Molly Asthore.

(Irish Song.)

SIR SAMUEL FERGUSON.

OH, Mary dear, oh, Mary fair,
    O branch of generous stem,
White blossom of the banks of Nair,
    Though lilies grow on them !
You've left me sick at heart for love,
    So faint I cannot see,
The candle swims the board above,
    I'm drunk for love of thee.
O stately stem of maiden pride,
    My woe it is, and pain,
That I, thus severed from thy side,
    The long night must remain !

Through all the towns of Inisfail
    I've wandered far and wide ;
But from Downpatrick to Kinsale,
    From Carlow to Kilbride,
'Mong lords and dames of high degree,
    Where'er my feet have gone,
My Mary, one to equal thee
    I've never looked upon ;
I live in darkness and in doubt
    Whene'er my love's away,
But were the blessed sun put out
    Her shadow would make day.

'Tis she indeed, young bud of bliss,
    And gentle as she's fair,
Though lily-white her bosom s,
    And sunny bright her hair,
And dewy-azure her blue eye,
    And rosy-red her cheek,
Yet brighter she in modesty,
    More beautifully meek.
The world's wise men from North to South
    Can never cure my pain ;
But one kiss from her honey mouth
    Would make me whole again !

Mild Mabel Kelly.

(Carolan.)

SIR SAMUEL FERGUSON.

WHOEVER the youth that by Heaven's decree
    Has his happy right hand 'neath that bright head
        of thine,
        'Tis certain that he
        From all sorrow is free
  Till the day of his death, if a life so divine
Should not raise him in bliss above mortal degree.
Mild Mabel-ni-Kelly, bright coolun of curls,
    All stately and pure as the swan on the lake ;
Her mouth of white teeth is a palace of pearls,
    And the youth of the land is love-sick for her sake !

No strain of the sweetest e'er heard in the land
    That she knows not to sing, in a voice so enchanting
        That the cranes on the strand
        Fall asleep where they stand ;
  Oh, for her blooms the rose, and the lily ne'er wanting
To shed its mild radiance o'er bosom or hand :
The dewy blue blossom that hangs on the spray,
    More blue than her eye, human eye never saw,
Deceit never lurked in its beautiful ray—
    Dear lady, I drink to you, *slainte go bragh !*

Pastheen Finn.

(Irish Rustic Song.)

SIR SAMUEL FERGUSON.

OH, my fair Pastheen is my heart's delight,
   Her gay heart laughs in her blue eye bright;
Like the apple-blossom her bosom white,
And her neck like the swan's on a March morn bright.

Chor.—Then, Oro, come with me! come with me! come
         with me!
      Oro, come with me! brown girl, sweet!
      And oh! I would go through snow and sleet,
      If you would come with me, brown girl, sweet!

Love of my heart, my fair Pastheen!
Her cheeks are red as the rose's sheen,
But my lips have tasted no more, I ween,
Than the glass I drank to the health of my queen!

Were I in the town where's mirth and glee,
Or 'twixt two barrels of barley bree,
With my fair Pastheen upon my knee,
'Tis I would drink to her pleasantly!

Nine nights I lay in longing and pain,
Betwixt two bushes, beneath the rain,
Thinking to see you, love, again ;
But whistle and call were all in vain !

I'll leave my people, both friend and foe ;
From all the girls in the world I'll go ;
But from you, sweetheart, oh, never ! oh, no !
Till I lie in the coffin stretched cold and low !

‌Pearl of the White Breast.

(From the Irish.)

GEORGE PETRIE.

THERE'S a colleen fair as May,
    For a year and for a day
I've sought by every way her heart to gain.
There's no art of tongue or eye
Fond youths with maidens try,
But I've tried with ceaseless sigh, yet tried in vain.
If to France or far-off Spain
She'd cross the watery main,

To see her face again the sea I'd brave.
And if 'tis Heaven's decree
That mine she may not be
May the Son of Mary me in mercy save !

O thou blooming milk-white dove,
To whom I've given true love,
Do not ever thus reprove my constancy.
There are maidens would be mine,
With wealth in hand and kine,
If my heart would but incline to turn from thee.
But a kiss with welcome bland,
And a touch of thy dear hand
Are all that I demand, would'st thou not spurn ;
For if not mine, dear girl,
O Snowy-Breasted Pearl !
May I never from the fair with life return !

Cashel of Munster.

(From the Irish.)

EDWARD WALSH.

I WOULD wed you, dear, without gold or gear, or
    counted kine,
My wealth you'll be, would your friends agree, and you
    be mine.
My grief, my gloom! that you do not come, my heart's
    dear hoard!
To Cashel fair though our couch were there but a soft
    deal board.

O come, my bride, o'er the wild hill-side to the valley
    low!
A downy bed for my love I'll spread where waters flow,
And we shall stray where streamlets play, the groves
    among,
Where echo tells to the listening dells the blackbird's
    song.

Love tender, true, I gave to you, and secret sighs,
In hope to see upon you and me one hour arise,
When the priest's blest voice would bind my choice and
    the ring's strict tie,
If wife you be, love, to one but me, love, in grief I'll
    die!

A neck of white has my heart's delight, and breast like
    snow,
And flowing hair whose ringlets fair to the green grass
    flow,
Alas ! that I did not early die, before the day
That saw me here, from my bosom's dear, far, far away !

The Maid of Ballyhaunis.

(From the Irish.)

EDWARD WALSH.

MY Mary, dear, for thee I die !
    Oh, place thy hand in mine, Love.
My fathers here were chieftains high,
    Then to my plaints incline, Love.
O Plaited-Hair ! that now we were
    In wedlock's band united !
For, maiden mine, in grief I'll pine
    Until our vows are plighted.

Thou, Rowan-Bloom, since thus I rove
    All worn and faint to greet thee,
Come to these arms, my constant love,
    With love as true to meet me !

Alas! my head, its wits are fled,
    I've failed in filial duty;
My sire did say, "Shun, shun, for aye
    That Ballyhaunis beauty!"

But thy *cúilin bán* [1] I marked one day,
    Where the blooms of the bean-field cluster,
Thy bosom white like ocean's spray,
    Thy cheeks like rowan-fruit's lustre.
Thy tones that shame the wild bird's fame
    Who sings in the Summer weather;
And oh, I sigh that thou and I
    Steal not from this world together!

If with thy love thou wilt depart
    To the Land of Ships, my fair Love!
No weary pain of head or heart
    Shall haunt our slumbers there, Love!
Oh, haste away, ere cold Death's prey
    My soul from thine withdrawn is!
And my hope's reward, the churchyard sward
    In the town of Ballyhaunis!

[1] Fair flowing hair.

Kitty Bhan.

(From the Irish.)

EDWARD WALSII.

BEFORE the sun rose at yester-dawn
  I met a fair maid adown the lawn ;
The berry and snow to her cheek gave its glow,
And her bosom was fair as the sailing swan.
Then, pulse of my heart ! what gloom is thine ?

IIer beautiful voice more hearts hath won
Than Orpheus' lyre of old hath done ;
IIer ripe eyes of blue were crystals of dew,
On the grass of the lawn before the sun.
And, pulse of my heart ! what gloom is thine ?

From the Cold Sod that's O'er You.

(From the Irish.)

EDWARD WALSH.

FROM the cold sod that's o'er you
    I never shall sever ;
Were my hands twined in yours, Love,
    I'd hold them for ever.
My fondest, my fairest,
    We may now sleep together !
I've the cold earth's damp odour,
    And I'm worn from the weather.

This heart filled with fondness
    Is wounded and weary ;
A dark gulf beneath it
    Yawns jet-black and dreary.
When death comes, a victor,
    In mercy to greet me,
On the wings of the whirlwind
    In the wild wastes you'll meet me.

When the folk of my household
    Suppose I am sleeping,
On your cold grave till morning
    The lone watch I'm keeping.

My grief to the night-wind,
   For the mild maid to render,
Who was my betrothed
   Since infancy tender.

Remember the lone night
   I last spent with you, Love,
Beneath the dark sloe-tree,
   When the icy wind blew, Love.
High praise to the Saviour !
   No sin stain had found you,
That your virginal glory
   Shines brightly around you.

The priests and the friars
   Are ceaselessly chiding,
That I love a young maiden
   In life not abiding.
Oh, I'd shelter and shield you
   If wild storms were swelling !
And oh, my wrecked hope,
   That the cold earth's your dwelling !

Beloved of the Flaxen Tresses.

(From the Irish.)

EDWARD WALSH.

AT Ballinahinch, my dear,
  Abides this long, long year,
    Than the Summer sun more brightly shining ;
Where'er her footsteps go,
Fair honey-flowers will grow,
    Even though 'twere Winter's dark declining.
If to my net she sped,
'Twould ease my heart and head,
    Where cruel Love his burning brand impresses.
From all that living be,
I'll choose no mate but thee,
    Beloved of the flaxen tresses !

At the bridge of the Avonmore
I saw my bosom's store,
    The maiden of the ringlets yellow ;
More sweet her kisses be
Than honey from the tree,
Or festive Spanish wine, of flavour mellow.

Her bosom, globes of white,
Sweet, fragrant, perfect, bright,
   Like drifted snow the mountain's heart that presses.
The cuckoo's notes resound
In Winter where thou'rt found,
   Beloved of the flaxen tresses !

Oh, if the boon were mine,
From beauty's ranks divine,
   To choose for aye the fairest maiden,
'Twere her to whom sweet lays
Consign the palm of praise,
   For whom a thousand hearts with love are laden.
Such maid did once inspire
The Hebrew monarch's lyre.
   But oh, thine eye more dignity expresses !
Believe my woe, I crave.
Oh, snatch me from the grave,
   Beloved of the flaxen tresses !

Little Celia Connellan.

(From the Irish.)

EDWARD WALSH.

OH, pearl-decked beauteous Celia,
    My first love of mildness rare,
My life full fast is fading,
    My soul is weary, vexed with care !
Come, snowy-bosomed maiden,
    And rove with me the valleys deep,
Or darkest gloom shall seize me,
    Till in the pitying grave I sleep !

Come, place the cups before us,
    Let choicest wines their brims o'erflow ;
We'll drown in draughts oblivious,
    The memory of her breast of snow ;
Her neck that's softer, fairer,
    Than silk or plumes of snowy white ;
For memory wild pursues her
    When severed from my longing sight !

Were thou and I, dear Smooth-neck !
Of mild cheek and bosom white,
In a summer vale of sweetness
  Reposing through the beauteous night !
No living thing around us
  But heath-cocks wild till break of dawn.
Oh, the sunlight of my bosom
  Were little Celia Connellan !

Mo Craoibhin Cno.[1]

EDWARD WALSH.

M Y heart is far from Liffey's tide
  And Dublin town ;
It strays beyond the Southern side
  Of Knockmeledown.
Where Cappoquin hath woodlands green,
  Where *Amhan-Mhor's* waters flow,
Where dwells unsung, unsought, unseen,
  Mo Craoibhin Cno !
Low clustering in her leafy screen,
  Mo Craoibhin Cno !

---

[1] Pronounced *ma creeveen O*—literally, *my cluster oj nuts*—that is, *my nut-brown maid.*

The high-bred dames of Dublin town
    Are rich and fair,
With wavy plume and silken gown,
    And stately air ;
Can plumes compare thy dark brown hair ?
    Can silk thy neck of snow ?
Or measured pace thine artless grace ?
    Mo Craoibhin Cno !
When harebells scarcely show thy trace,
    Mo Craoibhin Cno !

I've heard the songs by Liffey's wave
    That maidens sung,
They sung their land, the Saxon's slave,
    In Saxon tongue.
Oh, bring me here that Gaelic dear
    Which cursed the Saxon foe,
When thou didst charm my raptured ear,
    Mo Craoibhin Cno !
And none but God's good angels near,
    Mo Craoibhin Cno !

I've wandered by the rolling Lee
    And Lene's green bowers,
I've seen the Shannon's wide-spread sea
    And Limerick's towers,
And Liffey's tide, where halls of pride
    Frown o'er the flood below ;
My wild heart strays to *Amhan-Mhor's* side,
    Mo Craoibhin Cno !
With love and thee for aye to bide,
    Mo Craoibhin Cno !

Fairy Mary Barry.

(From the Irish.)

DR. GEORGE SIGERSON.

OH, Fairy Mary Barry, I tarry down-hearted ;
    Unknown to friend or kin, health and wealth have
      departed ;
When I'm going to my bed or I wake in the morning,
My thought is still of you and your cruel, cruel scorning.

Oh, Fairy Mary Barry, take counsel, my bright Love,
And send away the stranger from out of your sight, Love,
With all his fine airs, but there's more truth in me, Love,
And come to me, machree, since our parents agree, Love.

I thought I could coax you with promise and kisses,
I thought I could coax you with vows and caresses,
I thought I could coax you ere yellowed the barley,
But you've left me to the new year in sore sorrow fairly.

'Tis delight to the earth when your little feet press it,
'Tis delight to the earth when your sweet singings bless it,
'Tis delight to the earth when you lie, Love, upon it ;
But, oh, his delight who your heart, Love, has won it !

I would wander through the streets hand in hand with my
   true love;
I would sail the salt sea with no fortune but you, Love;
My nearest and dearest I'd leave them for ever,
And you'd call me from death if you said, "We'll ne'er
   sever."

I gave you my true love, I gave you my whole love;
On the festival of Mary my poor heart you stole, Love.
With your soft green eyes like dewdrops on corn newly
   springing,
And the music of your red lips like sweet starlings singing!

Were You on the Mountain?

(From the Irish.)

DOUGLAS HYDE.

OH, were you on the mountain, or saw you my love?
   Or saw you my own one, my queen and my dove?
Or saw you the maiden with the step firm and free?
And say, is she pining in sorrow like me?

I was upon the mountain, and saw there your love
I saw there your own one, your queen and your dove ;
I saw there the maiden with the step firm and free
And she was *not* pining in sorrow like thee.

The Outlaw of Loch Lene.

(From the Irish.)

J. J. CALLANAN.

OH, many a day have I made good ale in the glen,
    That came not of stream or malt—like the brewing
      of men,
My bed was the ground ; my roof the green wood above,
And the wealth that I sought, one far, kind glance from
    my Love.

Alas, on that night when the horses I drove from the
    field,
That I was not near my angel from terror to shield,
She stretched forth her arms—her mantle she flung to
    the wind,
And swam o'er Loch Lene her outlawed lover to find.

O would that the freezing sleet-winged tempest did sweep,
And I and my Love were alone, far off on the deep ;
I'd ask not a ship, or a bark, or pinnace to save,
With her hand round my waist I'd fear not the wind or
the wave.

'Tis down by the lake where the wild tree fringes its
sides,
The maid of my heart, my fair one of heaven, resides ;
I think as at eve she wanders its mazes along,
The birds go to sleep by the wild, sweet twist of her
song.

The Girl I Love.

J. J. CALLANAN.

THE girl I love is comely, straight, and tall ;
Down her white neck her auburn tresses fall ;
Her dress is neat, her carriage light and free,
Here's a health to that charming maid, whoe'er she be !

c*

The rose's blush but fades beside her cheek ;
Her eyes are blue, her forehead pale and meek ;
Her lips like cherries on a summer tree—
Here's a health to that charming maid, whoe'er she be !

When I go to the field no youth can lighter bound,
And I freely pay when the cheerful jug goes round ;
The barrel is full ; but its heart we soon shall see—
Come, here's to that charming maid, whoe'er she be !

Had I the wealth that props the Saxon's reign,
Or the diamond crown that decks the King of Spain,
I'd yield them all if she kindly smiled on me—
Here's a health to the maid I love, whoe'er she be !

Five pounds of gold for each lock of her hair I'd pay,
And five times five for my love one hour each day ;
Her voice is more sweet than the thrush on its own green
    tree !
Then, my dear, may I drink a fond, deep health to thee !

The Boatman of Kinsale.

THOMAS DAVIS.

HIS kiss is sweet, his word is kind,
    His love is rich to me ;
I could not in a palace find
    A truer Love than he.
The eagle shelters not his nest
    From hurricane and hail
More bravely than he guards my breast,
    The Boatman of Kinsale.

The wind that round the Fastnet sweeps
    Is not a whit more pure,
The goat that down Knock Sheehy leaps
    Has not a foot more sure.
No firmer hand nor freer eye
    E'er faced an autumn gale.
De Courcy's heart is not so high,
    The Boatman of Kinsale.

The brawling squires may heed him not
    The dainty stranger sneer,
But who will dare to hurt our cot
    When Myles O'Hea is here ?

The scarlet soldiers pass along,
    They'd like but fear to rail—
His blood is hot, his blow is strong,
    The Boatman of Kinsale.

His hooker's in the Scilly van
    When seines are in the foam ;
But money never made the man,
    Nor wealth a happy home.
So blest with love and liberty,
    While he can trim a sail,
He'll trust in God, and cling to me,
    The Boatman of Kinsale.

The Girl of Dunbwy.

THOMAS DAVIS.

'TIS pretty to see the girl of Dunbwy
    Stepping the mountain statelily,
Though ragged her gown and naked her feet,
No lady in Ireland to match her is meet.

Poor is her diet, and hardly she lies,
Yet a monarch might kneel for a glance of her eyes ;
The child of a peasant, yet England's proud queen
Has less rank in her heart, and less grace in her mien,

Her brow 'neath her raven hair gleams, just as if
A breaker spread white 'neath a shadowy cliff,
And love and devotion and energy speak
From her beauty-proud eye and her passion-pale cheek.

But pale as her cheek is there's pink on her lip,
And her teeth flash as white as the crescent moon's tip,
And her form and her step like the red deer's go past
As lightsome, as lovely, as haughty, as fast.

I saw her but once, and I looked in her eye,
And she knew that I worshipped her passing her by ;
The saint of the wayside, she granted my prayer,
Though we spoke not a word, for her mother was there.

I never can think upon Bantry's bright hills
But her image starts up, and my longing eye fills ;
And I whisper her softly, " Again, love, we'll meet,
And I'll lie in your bosom, and live at your feet."

ᵡ *Come to Me, Dearest.*

JOSEPH BRENNAN.

COME to me, dearest, I'm lonely without you;
  Day-time and night-time I'm thinking about you;
Night-time and day-time in dreams I behold you;
Unwelcome the waking which ceases to fold you.
Come to me, darling, my sorrows to lighten,
Come in your beauty to bless and to brighten;
Come in your womanhood, meekly and lowly,
Come in your lovingness, queenly and holy.

Swallows will flit round the desolate ruin,
Telling of Spring and its joyous renewing;
And thoughts of your love and its manifold treasure,
Are circling my heart with a promise of pleasure.
O Spring of my spirit, O May of my bosom,
Shine on my soul till it burgeon and blossom!
The waste of my life has a rose root within it,
And your fondness alone to the sunshine can win it.

You have been glad when you knew I was gladdened;
Dear, are you sad now to hear I am saddened?
Our hearts ever answer in tune and in time, Love,
As octave to octave, and rhyme unto rhyme, Love.
I cannot weep but your tears will be flowing;
You cannot smile but my cheeks will be glowing;
I would not die without you at my side, Love;
You will not linger when I shall have died, Love.

Come to me, dear, ere I die of my sorrow ;
Rise on my gloom like the sun of to-morrow ;
Strong, swift and fond as the words that I speak, Love,
With a song on your lips and a rose on your cheek,
    Love !
Come, for my heart in your absence is weary !
Come, for my spirit is sickened and dreary !
Come to the arms which alone should caress you
Come to the heart that is throbbing to press you !

Kitty Neil.

JOHN FRANCIS WALLER.

" AH, sweet Kitty Neil, rise up from your wheel,
    Your neat little foot will be weary of spinning
Come, trip with me down to the sycamore tree,
  Half the parish is there, and the dance is beginning.
The sun is gone down, but the full harvest moon
  Shines sweetly and cool in the dew-whitened valley ;
While all the air rings with the soft loving things
  Each little bird sings in the green shaded alley."

With a blush and a smile, Kitty rose up, the while
   Her eye in the glass, as she bound her hair, glancing ;
'Tis hard to refuse when a young lover sues,
   So she couldn't but choose to go off to the dancing.
And now on the green the glad groups are seen,
   Each gay-hearted lad with the lass of his choosing,
And Pat, without fail, leads out sweet Kitty Neil,
   Somehow when she asked he ne'er thought of refusing.

Now Felix Magee puts his pipes to his knee,
   And with flourish so free sets each couple in motion,
With a cheer and a bound the lads patter the ground,
   And the maids move around just like swans on the
      ocean !
Cheeks bright as the rose, feet light as the doe's,
   Now coyly retiring, now boldly advancing,
Search the world all around, from the sky to the ground,
   No such sight can be found as an Irish lass dancing !

Sweet Kate, who could view your bright eyes of deep
    blue
Beaming humidly through the dark lashes so mildly,
Your fair-turned arm, heaving breast, rounded form,
   Nor feel his heart warm, and his pulses throb wildly?
Young Pat feels his heart, as he gazes, depart,
   Subdued by the smart of such painful yet sweet love ;
The sight leaves his eye, as he cries, with a sigh,
   " Dance light, for my heart it lies under your feet,
    Love,"

Aileen.

JOHN BANIM.

'TIS not for love of gold I go,
　　'Tis not for love of fame ;
Though Fortune should her smile bestow,
　　And I may win a name,
　　　Aileen,
　　And I may win a name.

And yet it is for gold I go,
　　And yet it is for fame,
That they may deck another brow,
　　And bless another name,
　　　Aileen,
　　And bless another name.

For this, but this, I go, for this
　　I lose thy love awhile ;
And all the soft and quiet bliss
　　Of thy young, faithful smile,
　　　Aileen,
　　Of thy young, faithful smile.

And I go to brave a world I hate,
And woo it o'er and o'er
And tempt a wave, and try a fate
Upon a stranger shore,
Aileen,
Upon a stranger shore.

Oh, when the bays are all my own,
I know a heart will care !
Oh, when the gold is wooed and won,
I know a brow shall wear,
Aileen,
I know a brow shall wear !

And when with both returned again,
My native land to see,
I know a smile will meet me there,
And a hand will welcome me,
Aileen,
A hand will welcome me !

The Irish Wife.

(Earl Desmond's Apology. [1]

THOMAS D'ARCY MAGEE.

I WOULD not give my Irish wife
　　For all the dames of the Saxon land;
I would not give my Irish wife
　　For the Queen of France's hand;
For she to me is dearer
　　Than castles strong, or lands, or life—
An outlaw, so I'm near her,
　　To love till death my Irish wife.

Oh, what would be this home of mine?
　　A ruined, hermit-haunted place,
But for the light that still will shine
　　Upon its walls from Kathleen's face!
What comfort in a mine of gold?
　　What pleasure in a royal life?
If the heart within lay dead and cold,
　　If I could not wed my Irish wife.

---

[1] In 1376 the Statute of Kilkenny forbade the English settlers in Ireland to intermarry with the Irish under pain of outlawry. James, Earl of Desmond, was one of the first to violate this law. He was an accomplished poet.

I knew the laws forbade the banns,
   I knew my King abhorred her race
Who never bent before their clans
   Must bow before their ladies' grace.
Take all my forfeited domain,
   I cannot wage with kinsmen strife
Take knightly gear and noble name,
   And I will keep my Irish wife.

My Irish wife has clear blue eyes,
   My heaven by day, my stars by night,
And, twin-like, truth and fondness lie
   Within her swelling bosom white.
My Irish wife has golden hair—
   Apollo's harp had once such strings,
Apollo's self might pause to hear
   Her bird-like carol when she sings.

I would not give my Irish wife
   For all the dames of the Saxon land ;
I would not give my Irish wife
   For the Queen of France's hand.
For she to me is dearer
   Than castles strong, or lands, or life ;
In death I would lie near her,
   And rise beside my Irish wife.

Memories.

THOMAS D'ARCY MAGEE.

I LEFT two Loves on a distant strand,
  One fair and young and white of hand,
One fair and old and sadly grand,
My wedded wife and my native land.

One tarrieth sad and seriously
Beneath the roof that mine should be;
One sitteth sibyl-like by the sea,
Chanting a grave song mournfully.

A little life I have not seen
Lies by the heart that mine hath been
A cypress wreath darkles now, I ween,
Over the brow of my Love in green.

The mother and wife shall pass away,
Her hands be dust, her lips be clay;
But my other Love on earth shall stay
And live in the life of a better day.

Ere we were born my first Love was,
My sires were heirs to her holy cause;
And she yet shall sit in the world's applause,
A mother of men and blessed laws.

I hope and strive the while I sigh,
For I know my first Love cannot die ;
From the chain of woes that loom so high
Her reign shall reach to Eternity.

I Love my Love in the Morning.

GERALD GRIFFIN.

I LOVE my Love in the morning,
    For she like morn is fair—
Her blushing cheek its crimson streak,
    Its clouds her golden hair,
Her glance its beam so soft and kind,
    Her tears its dewy showers,
And her voice the tender whispering wind
    That stirs the early bowers.

I love my Love in the morning,
    I love my Love at noon,
For she is bright as the lord of light,
    Yet mild as Autumn's moon.
Her beauty is my bosom's sun,
    Her faith my fostering shade,
And I will love my darling one
    Till ever the sun shall fade.

I love my Love in the morning,
 I love my Love at even ;
Her smile's soft play is like the ray
 That lights the western heaven.
I loved her when the sun was high,
 I loved her when he rose,
But best of all when evening's sigh
 Was murmuring at its close.

The Lover and Birds.

WILLIAM ALLINGHAM.

WITHIN a budding grove,
 In April's ear sang every bird his best.
But not a song to pleasure my unrest,
 Or touch the tears unwept of bitter love ;
Some spake, methought, with pity, some as if in jest.
  To every word
  Of every bird
I listen'd, and replied as it behove.

Scream'd Chaffinch, "Sweet, sweet, sweet!
Pretty lovey, come and meet me here!"
"Chaffinch," quoth I, "be dumb awhile, in fear
    Thy darling prove no better than a cheat,
And never come, or fly when wintry days appear."
        Yet from a twig,
        With voice so big,
    The little fowl his utterance did repeat.

    Then I, " The man forlorn,
Hears Earth send up a foolish noise aloft."
" And what 'll *he* do ?   What 'll *he* do ? " scoff'd
    The Blackbird standing, in an ancient thorn,
Then spread his sooty wings and flitted to the croft,
        With cackling laugh ;
        Whom I, being half
Enraged, called after, giving back his scorn.

    Worse mock'd the Thrush, " Die ! die !
Oh, could he do it ? could he do it ?   Nay !
Be quick ! be quick !   Here, here, here ! " (went his lay.)
    "Take heed ! take heed !" then, "Why? why?
        why? why? why?
See-ee now ! see-ee now ! " (he drawled) " Back ! back
back !   R-r-r-run away ! "
        O Thrush, be still !
        Or at thy will
Seek some less sad interpreter than I.

"Air, air! blue air and white!
Whither I flee, whither, O whither, O whither I flee!"
(Thus the Lark hurried, mounting from the lea)
    "Hills, countries, many waters glittering bright
Whither I see, whither I see! deeper, deeper, deeper,
    whither I see, see, see!"
                "Gay Lark," I said,
                "The song that's bred
In happy nest may well to heaven make flight."

    "There's something, something sad
I half remember," piped a broken strain.
Well sung, sweet Robin! Robin sung again.
    "Spring's opening cheerily, cheerily! be we glad!"
Which moved, I wist not why, me melancholy mad,
                Till now, grown meek,
                With wetted cheek,
Most comforting and gentle thoughts I had.

Among the Heather.

WILLIAM ALLINGHAM.

ONE evening walking out I o'ertook a modest *colleen*,
    When the wind was blowing cool, and the harvest
        leaves were falling.

D

" Is our road, by chance, the same ?   Might we travel on
    together ?''
" Oh, I keep the mountain-side (she replied) among the
    heather."

" Your mountain air is sweet when the days are long and
    sunny,
When the grass grows round the rocks, and the whin-
    bloom smells like honey ;
But the winter's coming fast, with its foggy, snowy
    weather,
And you'll find it bleak and chill on your hill among the
    heather."

She praised her mountain home ; and I'll praise it too,
    with reason,
For where Molly is, there's sunshine and flow'rs at every
    season.
Be the moorland black or white, does it signify a feather,
Now I know the way by heart, every part, among the
    heather ?

The sun goes down in haste, and the night falls thick and
    stormy ;
Yet I'd travel twenty miles to the welcome that's before
    me ;
Singing hi for Eskydun, in the teeth of wind and weather !
Love'll warm me as I go through the snow, among the
    heather.

Lovely Mary Donnelly.

WILLIAM ALLINGHAM.

OH, LOVELY Mary Donnelly, my joy, my only best!
　If fifty girls were round you, I'd hardly see the rest ;
Be what it may the time o' day, the place be where it will,
Sweet looks o' Mary Donnelly, they bloom before me
　still.

Her eyes like mountain water that's flowing on a rock,
How clear they are, how dark they are ! they give me
　many a shock ;
Red rowans warm in sunshine and wetted with a shower,
Could ne'er express the charming lip that has me in its
　pow'r.

Her nose is straight and handsome, her eyebrows lifted
　up ;
Her chin is very neat and pert, and smooth like a china
　cup ;
Her hair's the brag of Ireland, so weighty and so fine ;
It's rolling down upon her neck, and gather'd in a twine.

The dance o' last Whit-Monday night exceeded all before ;
No pretty girl for miles about was missing from the
　floor ;
But Mary kept the belt o' love, and O but she was gay !
She danced a jig, she sung a song, that took my heart
　away !

When she stood up for dancing, her steps were so com-
        plete,
The music nearly killed itself to listen to her feet ;
The fiddler moan'd his blindness, he heard her so much
        praised,
But bless'd his luck to not be deaf when once her voice
        she raised.

And evermore I'm whistling or lilting what you sung,
Your smile is always in my heart, your name beside my
        tongue ;
But you've as many sweethearts as you'd count on both
        your hands,
And for myself there's not a thumb or little finger stands.

'Tis you're the flower o' womankind in country or in town !
The higher I exalt you, the lower I'm cast down.
If some great lord should come this way and see your
        beauty bright,
And you to be his lady, I'd own it was but right.

O might we live together in a lofty palace hall,
Where joyful music rises, and where scarlet curtains fall !
O might we live together in a cottage mean and small,
With sods o' grass the only roof, and mud the only wall !

O lovely Mary Donnelly, your beauty's my distress ;
It's far too beauteous to be mine, but I'll never wish it
        less.
The proudest place would fit your face, and I am poor
        and low ;
But blessings be about you, dear, wherever you may go !

Oh! Were my Love.

WILLIAM ALLINGHAM.

OH! were my Love a country lass,
  That I might see her every day,
And sit with her on hedgerow grass
  Beneath a bough of may;
And find her cattle when astray,
  Or help to drive them to the field,
And linger on our homeward way,
  And woo her lips to yield
A twilight kiss before we parted,
Full of love, yet easy-hearted.

Oh! were my Love a cottage maid,
  To spin through many a winter night,
Where ingle-corner lends its shade
  From fir-wood blazing bright.
Beside her wheel, what dear delight
  To watch the blushes go and come,
With tender words, that took no fright
  Beneath the friendly hum;
Or rising smile, or tear-drop swelling,
At a fireside legend's telling.

Oh ! were my Love a peasant girl,
        That never saw the wicked town ;
Was never dight with silk or pearl,
        But graced a homely gown.
How little force in fashion's frown
        To vex our unambitious lot ;
How rich were love and peace to crown
        Our green secluded cot ;
Where Age would come serene and shining
Like an autumn day's declining.

Song.

AUBREY DE VERE.

PHŒBUS paced the wooded mountain ;
        Kindled dawn, and met a doe.
" Child, what ails thee that thou rovest
        O'er my bright hills sad and slow ?

" That upon thy left side only
        Thou thy noontide sleep dost take ?
That thy foot the fountain troubles
        Ever ere thy thirst thou slake ? "

Answered then the weeping creature :
"Once beside me raced a fawn.
Seest her, O thou God all-seeing,
　O'er thy hills in wood or lawn ?

"On my left side sleep I only,
　For 'tis there my anguish stirs ;
And my foot the fountain troubles,
　Lest it yield me shape like hers."

Then the Sun-God marvelled, musing :
　"When my foolish Daphne died,
Rooted 'mid Peneian laurels,
　Scarce one little hour I sighed."

Song.

AUBREY DE VERE.

SLANTING both hands against her forehead,
　On me she levelled her bright eyes :
　　My whole heart brightened as the sea
　　When midnight clouds part suddenly ;
Through all my spirit went the lustre
　Like starlight poured through purple skies.

And then she sang a loud, sweet music,
  Yet louder as aloft it clomb ;
    Soft when her curving lips it left ;
    Then rising till the heavens were cleft,
As though each strain, on high expanding,
  Were echoed in a silver dome.

But ah ! she sings she does not love me ;
  She loves to say she ne'er can love ;
    To me her beauty she denies,
    Bending the while on me those eyes
Whose beams might charm the mountain leopard,
  Or lure Jove's herald from above !

Song.

AUBREY DE VERE.

SHE says : " Poor Friend, you waste a treasure
  Which you can ne'er regain—
Time, health, and glory, for the pleasure
  Of toying with a chain."
But then her voice so tender grows,
  So kind and so caressing ;
Each murmur from her lips that flows
  Comes to me like a blessing.

Sometimes she says : "Sweet Friend, I grieve you—
    Alas, it gives me pain !
What can I ? Ah, might I relieve you,
    You ne'er had mourned in vain !"
And then her little hand she presses
    Upon her heart, and sighs ;
While tears, whose source not yet she guesses,
    Grow larger in her eyes.

Florence MacCarthy's Farewell to his English Love.

AUBREY DE VERE.

MY pensive-browed Evangeline !
    What says to thee old Windsor's pine,
Whose shadow o'er the pleasaunce sways?
It says : "Ere long the evening star
Will pierce my darkness from afar.
    I grieve as one with grief who plays."

Evangeline ! Evangeline !
In that far-distant land of mine
    There stands a yew tree among tombs !
For ages there that tree has stood,
A black pall dashed with drops of blood ;
    O'er all my world it breathes its glooms

D*

England's fair child, Evangeline !
Because my yew-tree is not thine,
  Because thy gods on mine wage war,
Farewell ! Back fall the gates of brass ;
The exile to his own must pass—
  I seek the land of tombs once more.

Song.

AUBREY DE VERE.

GIVE me back my heart, fair child ;
  To you as yet 'twere worth but little !
Half beguiler, half beguiled,
  Be you warned : your own is brittle.

Hid it ? Dropt it on the moors ?
  Lost it, and you cannot find it ?
My own heart I want, not yours :
  You have bound, and must unbind it.

Fling it from you ! Youth is strong ;
  Love is trouble ; Love is folly.
Love, that makes an old heart young,
  Makes a young heart melancholy.

Minnie.

THOMAS CAULFIELD IRWIN.

O CRYSTAL Well,
   Play daintily on golden sands,
   When she comes at morning lonely,
   Followed by her shadow only,
  To bathe those little tender hands,
    All aweary gathering
    Seeds to make her blue bird sing.
O crystal Well !

O Forest brown,
   Breathe thy richest twilight balm,
   As she wanders, pulling willow
   Leaflets for her fragrant pillow,
  Which with snowy cheek and calm
    She shall press with half-closed eyes
    While the great stars o'er thee rise
O Forest brown !

O Lady Moon,
   Light her as she mounts the stair
    To her little sacred chamber
    Like a mother ; and remember
  While she slumbers full of prayer
    Sweetly then to fill her heart
    With dreams of heaven, where thou art
O Lady Moon !

My Ulick.

FRANCIS DAVIS.

MY Ulick is sturdy and strong,
    And light is his foot on the heather ;
And truth has been wed to his tongue
    Since first we were talking together ;
And though he is lord of no lands,
    Nor castle, nor cattle, nor dairy,
My boy has his health and his hands,
    And a heart-load of love for his Mary.
      And what should a maiden wish more ?

One day at the heel of the eve—
    I mind it was snowing and blowing—
My mother was knitting, I believe ;
    For me, I was singing and sewing ;
My father had read the news o'er,
    And as he sat humming, " We'll wake 'em
My Ulick stepped in at the door
    As white as the weather could make him.
      True love never cooled with a frost !

He shook the snow out of his frieze,
    And drew up a chair by my father.
My spirits leaped up in my eyes
    To see the two sitting together.

They talked of our land and its wrongs
  Till both were as mad as starvation ;
Then Ulick sang three or four songs,
  And closed with " Hurrah for *the Nation !* "
    Oh, Ulick's an Irishman still !

My father caught hold of his hand ;
  Their hearts melted into each other ;
While tears that she couldn't command
  Broke loose from the eyes of my mother.
" Our freedom," she sighed ; " wirrasthrue !
  A woman can say little in it ;
But had it to come by you two,
  I've a guess at the way we would win it.
    'Twould not be by weeping, I swear ! "

The Summer is Come.

ROBERT DWYER JOYCE.

THE summer is come and the grass is green,
  The gay flowers spring where the snow was seen,.
The ships are sailing upon the sea,
And I'll soon have tidings of Gra Machree.

Oh, weary weary, the long dull night
I sit and sigh for my heart's delight,
And in my dreaming see constantly
The stately form of my Gra Machree.

The birds are singing from brake and bough,
And sweetly, sweetly remind me now
Of the day we danced by the village tree,
When I won the heart of my Gra Machree.

But oh ! I'm sure, while the sunbeams glow
While flowers are springing and soft winds blow,
The white ships sailing upon the sea
Will soon bring tidings of Gra Machree.

The Wind that Shakes the Barley.

ROBERT DWYER JOYCE.

I SAT within the valley green,
　　I sat me with my true love.
My sad heart strove the two between—
　　The old love and the new love.

The old for her, the new that made
　Me think on Ireland dearly ;
While soft the wind blew down the glade,
　And shook the golden barley.

'Twas hard the woful words to frame,
　To break the ties that bound us ;
'Twas harder still to bear the shame
　Of foreign chains around us.
And so I said : "The mountain glen
　I'll seek at morning early,
And join the brave United men,"
　While soft winds shook the barley.

While sad I kissed away her tears,
　My fond arms round her flinging ;
The foeman's shot burst on our ears,
　From out the wildwood ringing ;
The bullet pierced my true love's side,
　In life's young Spring so early,
And on my breast in blood she died,
　When soft winds shook the barley.

But blood for blood without remorse
　I've ta'en at Oulart Hollow ;
I've placed my true love's clay-cold corse
　Where I full soon will follow ;

And round her grave I wander drear,
  Noon, night, and morning early.
With breaking heart whene'er I hear
  The wind that shakes the barley !

The Rejected Lover.

ALFRED PERCEVAL GRAVES.

ON Innisfallen's fairy isle,
    Amid the blooming bushes,
We leant upon the lover's stile,
    And listened to the thrushes ;
When first I sighed to see her smile,
    And smiled to see her blushes.

Her hair was bright as beaten gold,
    And soft as spider's spinning ;
Her cheek out-bloomed the apple old
    That set our parents sinning ;
And in her eyes you might behold
    My joys and griefs beginning.

In Innisfallen's fairy grove
  I hushed my happy wooing,
To listen to the brooding dove
  Amid the branches cooing ;
But oh ! how short those hours of love !
  How long their bitter rueing !

Poor cushat ! Thy complaining breast
  With woe like mine is heaving ;
With thee I mourn a fruitless quest—
  For ah ! with art deceiving,
The cuckoo-bird has robbed my nest,
  And left me wildly grieving.

'Twas Pretty to be in Ballinderry.

ALFRED PERCEVAL GRAVES.

'TWAS pretty to be in Ballinderry,
  'Twas pretty to be in Aghalee,
'Twas prettier to be in little Ram's Island,
  Trysting under the ivy tree !
    Ochone, ochone !
    Ochone, ochone !
For often I roved in little Ram's Island,
Side by side with Phelimy Hyland,
And still he'd court me, and I'd be coy,
Though at heart I loved him, my handsome boy !

" I'm going," he sighed, " from Ballinderry
    Out and across the stormy sea;
Then if in your heart you love me, Mary,
    Open your arms at last to me."
        Ochone, ochone !
        Ochone, ochone !
I opened my arms, how well he knew me !
I opened my arms and took him to me ;
And there in the gloom of the groaning mast
We kissed our first and we kissed our last.

'Twas happy to be in little Ram's Island,
    But now 'tis as sad as sad can be ;
For the ship that sailed with Phelimy Hyland
    Is sunk for ever beneath the sea.
        Ochone, ochone !
        Ochone, ochone !
And 'tis oh ! but I wear the weeping willow
And wander alone by the lonesome billow,
And cry to him over the cruel sea,
" Phelimy Hyland, come back to me ! "

The White Blossom's off the Bog.

ALFRED PERCEVAL GRAVES.

THE white blossom's off the bog and the leaves are
off the trees,
And the singing birds have scattered across the stormy
seas :
> And oh ! 'tis winter,
> Wild, wild winter !
With the lonesome wind sighing for ever through the
trees.

How green the leaves were springing ! how glad the birds
were singing !
When I rested in the meadow with my head on Patrick's
knees ;
> And oh ! 'twas spring-time,
> Sweet, sweet spring-time !
With the daisies all dancing before in the breeze.

With the spring the fresh leaves they'll laugh upon the
trees,
And the birds they'll flutter back with their songs across
the seas,
But I'll never rest again with my head on Patrick's
knees ;
> And for me 'twill be winter,
> All the year winter,
With the lonesome wind sighing for ever through the
trees!

Maire my Girl.

JOHN KEEGAN CASEY.

OVER the dim blue hills
    Strays a wild river ;
Over the dim blue hills
    Rests my heart ever.
Dearer and brighter than
    Jewels and pearl,
Dwells she in beauty there,
    Maire my girl.

Down upon Claris heath
    Shines the soft berry ;
On the brown harvest tree
    Droops the red cherry.
Sweeter thy honey lips,
    Softer the curl
Straying adown thy cheeks,
    Maire my girl.

'Twas on an April eve
    That I first met her ;
Many an eve shall pass
    Ere I forget her.

Since my young heart has been
    Wrapped in a whirl,
Thinking and dreaming of
    Maire my girl.

She is too kind and fond
    Ever to grieve me,
She has too pure a heart
    E'er to deceive me.
Were I Tyrconnel's Chief,
    Or Desmond's Earl,
Life would be dark without
    Maire my girl !

Over the dim blue hills
    Strays a wild river ;
Over the dim blue hills
    Rests my heart ever.
Dearer and brighter than
    Jewels or pearl,
Dwells she in beauty there,
    Maire my girl !

Gracie Og Machree.

(A Song of " the Wild Geese.")

JOHN KEEGAN CASEY.

I PLACED the silver in her palm,
　　By Inny's smiling tide,
And vowed ere summer-time came on
　　To claim her as a bride.
But when the summer-time came on,
　　I dwelt beyond the sea ;
Yet still my heart is ever true
　　To *Gracie Og Machree.*

Oh, bonny are the woods of Targ,
　　And green thy hills, Rathmore,
And soft the sunlight ever falls
　　On Darre's sloping shore ;
And there the eyes I love—in tears
　　Shine ever mournfully,
While I am far, and far away
　　From *Gracie Og Machree.*

When battle-steeds were neighing loud,
  With bright blades in the air,
Next to my inmost heart I wore
  A bright tress of her hair.
When stirrup-cups were lifted up
  To lips with soldier glee,
One toast I ever fondly pledged,
  'Twas *Gracie Og Machree.*

Oh, I may never, never clasp
  Again her snowy hand,
And I may find a soldier's grave
  Upon a foreign strand ;
But when the heart-pulse beats its last
  And death takes hold of me,
One word shall part my dying lips,
  Thy name, *Astor Machree.*

Song.

ARTHUR O'SHAUGHNESSY.

I MADE another garden, yea,
  For my new Love.
I left the dead rose where it lay
  And set the new above.

Why did my Summer not begin?
Why did my heart not haste?
My old Love came and walked therein
And laid the garden waste.

She entered with her weary smile,
Just as of old ;
She looked around a little while
And shivered with the cold.
Her passing touch was death to all,
Her passing look a blight ;
She made the white rose-petals fall,
And turned the red rose white.

Her pale robe clinging to the grass
Seemed like a snake
That bit the grass and ground, alas !
And a sad trail did make.
She went up slowly to the gate,
And then, just as of yore,
She turned back at the last to wait
And say farewell once more.

To God and Ireland True.

ELLEN O'LEARY.

I SIT beside my darling's grave
   Who in the prison died,
And though my tears fall thick and fast
   I think of him with pride :
Ay, softly fall my tears like dew,
For one to God and Ireland true.

"I love my God o'er all," he said,
   "And then I love my land,
And next I love my Lily sweet
   Who pledged me her white hand :
To each, to all, I'm ever true,
To God, to Ireland, and to you.

No tender nurse his hard bed smoothed,
   Or softly raised his head :
He fell asleep and woke in heaven
   Ere I knew he was dead ;
Yet why should I my darling rue ?
He was to God and Ireland true.

E

Oh, 'tis a glorious memory;
    I'm prouder than a queen
To sit beside my hero's grave
    And think on what has been :
And O my darling, I am true
To God, to Ireland, and to you !

After Aughrim.

ARTHUR GERALD GEOGHEGAN.

DO you remember long ago,
    Kathaleen ?
When your lover whispered low,
" Shall I stay or shall I go,
    Kathaleen ? "
And you answered proudly, " Go !
And join King James and strike a blow
    For the Green."

Mavrone, your hair is white as snow,
    Kathaleen ;
Your heart is sad and full of woe,
Do you repent you bade him go,
    Kathaleen ?
But quick you answer proudly, " No !
For better die with Sarsfield so,
Than live a slave without a blow
    For the Green."

Aghadoe.

JOHN TODHUNTER.

THERE'S a glade in Aghadoe, Aghadoe, Aghadoe,
  There's a green and silent glade in Aghadoe,
Where we met, my Love and I, Love's fair planet in the
    sky,
O'er that sweet and silent glade in Aghadoe.

There's a glen in Aghadoe, Aghadoe, Aghadoe,
  There's a deep and secret glen in Aghadoe,
Where I hid him from the eyes of the red-coats and their
    spies
That year the trouble came to Aghadoe.

Oh ! my curse on one black heart in Aghadoe, Aghadoe,
  On Shaun Dhuv, my mother's son in Aghadoe,
When your throat fries in hell's drouth salt the flame be in
    your mouth,
For the treachery you did in Aghadoe !

For they tracked me to that glen in Aghadoe, Aghadoe,
  When the price was on his head in Aghadoe ;
O'er the mountain through the wood, as I stole to him
    with food,
When in hiding lone he lay in Aghadoe.

But they never took him living in Aghadoe, Aghadoe ;
With the bullets in his heart in Aghadoe,
There he lay, the head—my breast keeps the warmth
    where once 'twould rest—
Gone, to win the traitor's gold from Aghadoe !

I walked to Mallow Town from Aghadoe, Aghadoe,
Brought his head from the gaol's gate to Aghadoe,
Then I covered him with fern and I piled on him the
    cairn,
Like an Irish king he sleeps in Aghadoe.

Oh, to creep into that cairn in Aghadoe, Aghadoe !
There to rest upon his breast in Aghadoe !
Sure your dog for you could die with no truer heart than
    I—
Your own love cold on your cairn in Aghadoe.

Girlhood at Midnight.

ROSA MULHOLLAND.

THOU art not coming, sleep ; then hie away,
    And let my leaping thoughts be quit of thee.
The moon hath teemed upon my chamber-floor—
A rain of tender light from Paradise ;

And round my casement, yawning to the blue,
The stirring, breathing passion-flowerets cling :
It is too fair a night to swoon away,
And lie unconscious till the lark's aloft !

From out my little bed I step herewith
And leave its gleaming whiteness in the shades ;
I will go forth and walk with shining feet
Under the moon, and hear the nightingales.
Jug, jug, tirroo, tirroo !   O sweet, my heart
But listen, listen to the voice of love,
Singing in dreams from out the gloom of leaves :
The red rose is awake and listening too !

O lady rose, O sister, fragrant, sweet,
Thou dost not know what now I tell thee, true,
That yesterday he likened me to thee,
And praised my damask cheek and called me fair.
Jug, jug, tirroo, tirroo ! he called me fair,
That ne'er was fair unto myself before ;
So I am safely housed within a heart,
O rose, as that dewdrop is housed in thine !

Now I have banished sleep, and come alive
To whisper thee my news in this still hour.
Thou and the moon, no other hath my tale ;
And mind thou dost not tell it to the sun,
Or any prying creature winging by.
My secret I will keep another day—
Then all the world can wonder at my joy.

Coming !

GEORGE NOBLE PLUNKETT.

HERE, where a sea of iris sweeps,
　　In tremulous circles swelling,
Rippled with joy,—as from its deeps
　　A fount of light were welling,
Now from thy home i' the setting sun,
　　Clothed in his glow, sweet rover,
Come ere the day's glad vision's gone,
　　And bless thy faithful lover !

The changeless calm ascetic heights
　　Are crowned with tender haloes,
The bold rocks burn with amber lights
　　Above the lapping shallows.
The olive takes a happier hue
　　Under the pine-shield's cover ;
And cloud-boats moored in waveless blue
　　Are waiting with thy lover !

Ah, what avail if the purple hill
　　The faun or nymph are haunting,
That great souls tread the wild shore still
　　If you should yet be wanting !
The Graces dwelling in flower and tree
　　For Love's eyes to discover,
Full of their smiling mystery,
　　Are waiting with thy lover.

Come, O my own, my only dear !
  Yet haply if I meet you,
Love on my cold lips white as fear,
  May lack true words to greet you.
You come ! Oh, see yon brood of doves
  Over you wheel and hover !
Clasp them and think, "those simple loves
  Fly from his heart, my lover!"

An Old Song Resung.

W. B. YEATS.

DOWN by the salley gardens my love and I did meet ;
  She passed the salley gardens with little snow-white feet.
She bid me take love easy as the leaves grow on the tree;
But I, being young and foolish, with her would not agree.

In a field by the river my love and I did stand,
And on my leaning shoulder she laid her snow-white hand.
She bid me take life easy as the grass grows on the weirs ;
But I was young and foolish, and now am full of tears.

To an Isle in the Water.

W. B. YEATS.

SHY one, shy one,
    Shy one of my heart,
She moves in the firelight,
    Pensively apart.

She carries in the dishes
    And lays them in a row.
To an isle in the water
    With her I would go.

She carries in the candles,
    And lights the curtained room ;
Shy in the doorway
    And shy in the gloom ;

And shy as a rabbit,
    Helpful and shy.
To an isle in the water
    With her would I fly.

Outside.

FRANCES WYNNE.

A SHINING pathway of light slopes down from the
half-closed door,
Through the darkness on either hand it glimmers
golden and wide,
A fair bridge spanning the night, and the dread desola-
tion o'er,
Stretching to me, where I stand forgotten, forlorn,
outside.

If I dared to turn my feet away from the chill and the
gloom,
If I followed yon radiant track with eager and noise-
less tread,
Should I find her, my only sweet, in some fragrant, fire-
lit room,
Her soft dress shadowy black, and the glow on her
bent bright head?

Perhaps, if I only dared, she would not bid me begone;
Perhaps she would smile as of yore, and be kind and
forget to chide;
Perhaps if she knew how I cared; I will go: I will seek
her anon;
Alas! they have shut the door and I am alone outside.

E*

Little Mary Cassidy.

FRANCIS A. FAHY.

OH, 'tis little Mary Cassidy's the cause of all my
    misery,
  And the raison that I am not now the boy I used
    to be;
Oh, she bates the beauties all that we read about in
    history,
  And sure half the country-side is as hot for her as
    me.
Travel Ireland up and down, hill, village, vale and
    town
  Fairer than the *Cailin Donn*, you're looking for in
    vain ;
Oh, I'd rather live in poverty with little Mary Cassidy
  Than emperor, without her, be of Germany or Spain.

'Twas at the dance at Darmody's that first I caught a
    sight of her,
  And heard her sing the *Droighncan Donn*, till tears
    came in my eyes,
And ever since that blessed hour I'm dreaming day
    and night of her;
  The divil a wink of sleep at all I get from bed to rise.

Cheeks like the rose in June, song like the lark in tune,
  Working, resting, night or noon, she never leaves my
    mind;
Oh, till singing by my cabin fire sits little Mary Cassidy,
  'Tis little aise or happiness I'm sure I'll ever find.

What is wealth, what is fame, what is all that people
    fight about
  To a kind word from her lips or a love-glance from
    her eye?
Oh, though troubles throng my breast, sure they'd soon
    go to the right-about
  If I thought the curly head of her would rest there by
    and by.
Take all I own to-day, kith, kin, and care away,
  Ship them all across the say, or to the frozen zone:
Lave me an orphan bare,—*but lave me Mary Cassidy*,
  I never would feel lonesome with the two of us alone.

The Wood-Pigeon.

KATHARINE TYNAN.

THE skies they were leaden, the snow-flakes were
    falling;
No blackbird or linnet was courting or calling;
But the wood-dove's sweet moaning was heard in the
    distance,
And her song all of love came in dulcet persistence.

Oh, what though the nests were all flooded with water,
And the cold eggs would give them no sweet son or
    daughter,
She was dreamy with pleasure for her true Love be-
    side her,
And her day was as gold as though young leaves did
    hide her!

O Love, sang the wood-dove, the sweet bird of Summer,
It were death, it were madness, were my Love a roamer;
But Love true and faithful, what power has cold weather
To still our wild songs, Love, since we are together?

Then I said to my true Love, true love is enough, Love,
And how wise is the wood-dove who learns that lore
    off, Love!
'Tis our charm for the Winter, and when the winds cry,
    Love,
And when, in the grave, on your heart I shall lie, Love.

A Irish Love-Song.

KATHARINE TYNAN.

WOULD God I were that tender apple-blossom,
    Floating and falling from the twisted bough,
To lie and faint within your silken bosom,
    As that does now!

Or would I were a little burnished apple
    For you to pluck me, gliding by so cold,
While sun and shade your robe of lawn will dapple,
    Your hair's spun gold.

Yea, would to God I were among the roses
    That lean to kiss you as you float between!
While on the lowest branch a bud uncloses
    To touch you, Queen!

Nay, since you will not love, would I were growing
    A happy daisy in the garden-path;
That so your silver foot might press me going,
    Even unto death!

An Errand.

JANE BARLOW.

I SLEPT; and where her lonely flower-knots gleam
    My dear lost Love I saw anear my side,
Yet knew our fate; since in my dreamiest dream
    How should I once forget that Norah died?

But by a blossomed briar methought she stood
    Whereon the rose's dawn was fair to see;
And: "Bend the spray," she said, "and this small bud
    It lifts so high above us, pluck for me.

"This is the flower I ever loved of yore,
    This little rose, that where its petals part
Is all a-flush within as if it bore
    A rosier rose's shadow at its heart."

Then, "O my love," I said, "needs must there be
    In thy dread world unwist of mortal eyes
Full many a wondrous bloom, and worthier thee
    Than aught that drinks the light of these dim skies!"

"Most fair," quoth she, "untouched of change that mars,
　　I see them shine; yet this I chide in all,
That steadfast bides their beauty as a star's,
　　Nor ever a glow will fade, a leaf will fall.

"For so, Beloved, I still have vainly sought,
　　And missed in sheeniest sheen, in sweetest sweet,
A symbol of the old life's bliss pain-fraught—
　　Thine yet—where all delight doth fail and fleet.

"Hence, for the old days' sake, from that far land
　　To clasp these flowers a weary way fare I,
Because their deathward drooping in my hand
　　Breathes memory of our love that shall not die."

On All Souls Night.

DORA SIGERSON.

O MOTHER, mother, I swept the hearth, I set his
　　chair and the white board spread,
I prayed for his coming to our kind Lady when Death's
　　sad doors would let out the dead;

A strange wind rattled the window-pane, and down the
    lane a dog howled on,
I called his name and the candle flame burnt dim, pressed
    a hand the door-latch upon.
Deelish ! Deelish ! my woe forever that I could not sever
    coward flesh from fear.
I called his name and the pale Ghost came ; but I was
    afraid to meet my dear.

O mother, mother, in tears I checked the sad hours past
    of the year that's o'er,
Till by God's grace I might see his face and hear the
    sound of his voice once more ;
The chair I set from the cold and wet, he took when he
    came from unknown skies
Of the land of the dead, on my bent brown head I felt
    the reproach of his saddened eyes ;
I closed my lids on my heart's desire, crouched by the
    fire, my voice was dumb.
At my clean-swept hearth he had no mirth, and at my
    table he broke no crumb.
Deelish ! Deelish ! my woe forever that I could not sever
    coward flesh from fear.
His chair put aside when the young cock cried, and I
    was afraid to meet my dear.

Index to Authors.

ALLINGHAM, WILLIAM. Born at Ballyshannon, 1824 ; died 1889. After contributing to *Athenæum*, *Household Words*, and other periodicals, he published his first volume, "Poems," in 1850. This was followed by several other volumes, and after his death Messrs. Reeves and Turner published his work in six volumes. Was for some years editor of *Fraser's Magazine*, through which ran his long narrative poem "Laurence Bloomfield in Ireland." He married, in 1850, Miss Helen Patterson, the well-known artist.

BANIM, JOHN. Born in Kilkenny, April 3, 1798 ; died, August 1, 1842. With his brother Michael, he wrote and published "Tales of the O'Hara Family," which rank only lower than Carleton's as delineations of Irish life and character. He wrote but a few poems, of which the best is "Soggarth Aroon." His drama, "Damon

113

and Pythias," was played in London in 1822, with
Kemble and Macready as the principal actors.

BARLOW, JANE. Daughter of the Rev. James Barlow,
a Fellow of Trinity College, Dublin. Has published
anonymously in magazines for some years dramatic
poems in the Irish dialect, which excited much admira-
tion and speculation as to the authorship. These have
recently appeared with other poems in a volume called
"Bog-Land Studies" (Fisher Unwin, London), and
have been received with the applause of the literary
journals. The book is a notable accession to Irish poetical
literature.

BRENAN, JOSEPH. Born in Cork, November 17, 1828;
died in New Orleans, May 27, 1857. Was a participator
in the National movement of '48, and imprisoned in
Kilmainham. After his release went to New York,
where he obtained employment as a journalist. After his
marriage in 1851, he joined the staff of the New Orleans
Delta. He never published a volume, but the few poems
of his that are accessible are of great beauty.

CALLANAN, JEREMIAH JOSEPH. Born at Cork, 1795;
died at Lisbon, 1829. Educated for the priesthood at
Maynooth, but because of delicate health gave up his
design. Entered Trinity College, Dublin, in 1820, but
remained only a few months. Was tutor under Dr.
Maginn, and, through him, became a writer for *Black-
wood*. In 1829 went as tutor to a family in Lisbon, but
died soon after going there.

CASEY, JOHN KEEGAN ("LEO"). The son of a
peasant. Born at Mullingar, 1846; died, 1870. Was
imprisoned as a Fenian, and died, it is said, from the

hardships then suffered. His poems are contained in a couple of little volumes published in Dublin during the Sixties.

DARLEY, GEORGE. Born in Dublin, 1785; died in London, 1846. Published "Sylvia; or, the May'Queen," "Errors of Ecstasie, and other Poems," and some dramas.

DAVIS, FRANCIS ("The Belfast Man"). Born in Ballincollig, co. Cork, 1810; died in Belfast, 1885. A weaver by trade. He published three volumes of verse, contributed to *The Nation*, and edited *The Belfastman's Journal*.

DAVIS, THOMAS OSBORNE. Born, October 14, 1814; died September 16, 1845. Educated at Trinity College, Dublin, where he graduated in 1836; he was called to the Bar two years later. One of the leaders of the '48 movement, and the noblest and most impressive figure of his time.

DE VERE, AUBREY. Born at Curragh Chase, co. Limerick, 1814. Has well been called "The Wearer of Wordsworth's Mantle."

FAHY, FRANCIS ("Dreolin"). A young poet with a genuine lyrical gift. Lives in London. Has published one volume of poems.

FERGUSON, SIR SAMUEL. Born in Belfast, 1810; died, 1886. Perhaps the most Irish of all our poets, and the author of the finest ballad in the Anglo-Irish literature, "The Vengeance of the Welshmen of Tyrawley."

GEOGHEGAN, ARTHUR. Born in Dublin, 1809; died in London, November, 1889. The author of "The Monks of Kilcrea," published by Bell and Daldy in 1861.

GRAVES, ALFRED PERCEVAL. Born in Dublin, 1846. Son of the Bishop of Limerick. Has published two volumes of Irish poems.

GRIFFIN, GERALD. Born in Limerick, 1803; died in Cork, 1840. Wrote dramas and novels, the best known of the latter being "The Collegians." Became a Christian Brother two years before his death, and died in the Order.

HYDE, DOUGLAS. Son of the Rector of Frenchpark, co. Roscommon. A Doctor of Laws of Trinity College, Dublin, and the most accomplished of young Irish scholars.

IRWIN, THOMAS CAULFIELD. Born at Warrenpoint, co. Down, 1823; died in Dublin, 1892. Contributed to *The Nation* in its palmy days, to *The Dublin University Magazine*, and other periodicals. Published several volumes of poems and stories in verse.

JOYCE, ROBERT DWYER. Born in co. Limerick, 1830; died Dublin, 1883. In 1866 emigrated to Boston, where he practiced his profession of medical man. Was author, besides his early volumes of Ballads, of "Deirdre" and "Blanid," two fine and picturesque poems on old Celtic stories.

MANGAN, JAMES CLARENCE. Esteemed the first of Irish poets. Born, 1803; died, 1849. His life is one long record of the struggle of genius with misery and ill-health —a gloomy and terrible story. Haverty, of New York, published a large but incomplete volume of his poems some years ago.

MCGEE, THOMAS D'ARCY. One of the '48 poets. Born, 1825, in Carlingford, co. Louth; murdered in Montreal, 1868.

MULHOLLAND, ROSA. Born in Belfast. A brilliant novelist; her contributions to poetry are too few. Her prose style is delicate and exquisite. She married, in 1891, Mr. J. T. Gilbert, the historian and antiquary.

OGLE, RIGHT HON. GEORGE. Born, 1739; died, 1814. Represented Dublin City in 1799, and voted against the Union.

O'LEARY, ELLEN. Born in Tipperary, 1831; died in Cork, 1889. Sister of the Fenian leader, John O'Leary. A small volume of her simple and beautiful poems has been published since her death.

O'SHAUGHNESSY, ARTHUR. Born, 1846; died, 1881. Published "Music and Moonlight," "An Epic of Women," and "Lays of France."

PETRIE, GEORGE. Born in Dublin, 1789; died, 1866. Artist and antiquary.

PLUNKETT, GEORGE NOBLE. Born in Dublin. Has published one small volume of poems. Edited *Hibernia*, and is now a barrister of Dublin.

REYNOLDS, GEORGE NUGENT. A favourite song-writer of the end of the last century.

SIGERSON, GEORGE. A medical doctor in Dublin, and Fellow and Professor of the Royal University. Translated a volume of Irish poems and has written some admirable original pieces.

SIGERSON, DORA. The young daughter of the above-named.

TODHUNTER, JOHN. Was formerly a physician in Dublin, but is now resident in London. Has published several volumes of poems and plays after the Greek manner.

WALSH, EDWARD. Born in 1805; died in 1850.

Lived in poor circumstances. A poet of undoubted genius.

WALLER, JOHN FRANCIS. Born, 1809.

WYNNE, FRANCES. A young writer of delightful poems. Her first little volume, published in 1890, won for her instant recognition.

YEATS, WILLIAM BUTLER. Born, 1865. The most notable of young Irish poets. Has published one volume, "The Wanderings of Oisin." A second, "The Countess Kathleen, and other Legends," has just been published.

The Gresham Press,

UNWIN BROTHERS,

CHILWORTH AND LONDON.